Upland
Bird Hunting

BY JENNY CROOKS-JOHNSON

childsworld.com

Published by The Child's World®
800-599-READ • www.childsworld.com

Photography Credits
Photographs ©: Delmas Lehman/Shutterstock Images, cover, 1; Steve Oehlenschlager/Shutterstock Images, 5, 15, 19; Matthew Crissall/iStockphoto, 6; Piotr Krzeslak/Shutterstock Images, 7 (top); Steve Oehlenschlager/iStockphoto, 7 (middle); Dennis W Donohue/Shutterstock Images, 7 (bottom); iStockphoto, 9, 17; Kozup Photography/Shutterstock Images, 11; Shutterstock Images, 13 (top), 13 (bottom); Jacob Boomsma/Shutterstock Images, 14; NS Images/iStockphoto, 20; CCPixx Photography/Shutterstock Images, 21

ISBN Information
9781503869752 (Reinforced Library Binding)
9781503881068 (Portable Document Format)
9781503882379 (Online Multi-user eBook)
9781503883680 (Electronic Publication)

LCCN 2022951186

Printed in the United States of America

ABOUT THE AUTHOR
Jenny Crooks-Johnson grew up in Wyoming with an upland game bird hunting dad and bird dogs as pets. These days she enjoys writing for children and exploring the Colorado outdoors with her amazing family.

CONTENTS

CHAPTER ONE

HUNTING DAY

It is a crisp November day. Liz and Ben jump out of the truck with their dad. They put on their boots, jackets, and hunting vests. Then they put on safety glasses, earplugs, and bright orange hats. Their dog Rex runs back and forth between them. "I guess I'm not the only one who's excited to hunt pheasants," says Liz. She makes sure the safety on her shotgun is on. This prevents the gun from firing accidentally. Then Liz loads **shotgun shells** into the shotgun.

Now it's time to hunt. Ben, Liz, and their dad walk behind Rex. They hold their shotguns straight up so the guns stay pointed away from the group. This keeps everyone safe. Rex zigzags back and forth, sniffing the tall prairie grasses. Rex's powerful nose soon catches a whiff of pheasant—a type of upland **game** bird.

"Look! Rex is on point!" Ben says. Rex is a German shorthaired pointer. He is a bird dog, or a dog trained for hunting. When a bird dog like Rex is on point, it means he is holding very still. His tail is straight back. His paw is lifted. His neck is stretched forward so his nose points toward the pheasant's smell. This lets Liz, Ben, and their dad know that a pheasant is nearby.

Many upland game birds can be found in prairies, farmlands, marshes, and crop fields.

Some hunters train their dogs to hunt birds. The most common types of bird dogs are retrievers, pointers, and spaniels (pictured).

Ben and Liz slowly move in front of Rex. They try to get the pheasant to **flush** out of the tall grasses. Then Rex points toward some bushes. There is a fence behind the bushes. If a pheasant is there, it can't run far.

COMMON UPLAND GAME BIRDS
IN THE UNITED STATES

Ring-necked Pheasant

Habitat: farmland, grassland, marshes, and bushes

Ruffed Grouse

Habitat: young hardwood forests

Bobwhite Quail

Habitat: farmland, brushland, and edges of woods

Common types of upland game birds in the United States include the ring-necked pheasant, the ruffed grouse, and the bobwhite quail.

Suddenly, a flutter of wings makes everyone jump. A colorful bird with a long tail bursts into the air. It's a male pheasant, or rooster. Ben and Liz quickly scan the area around the rooster to make sure there are no other dogs or hunters nearby. By checking their surroundings, they can make sure nobody gets hurt. Then Ben and Liz raise their shotguns to their shoulders and push their gun safeties off.

At first, the rooster is in Ben's safe **shooting zone**. But then it flies into Liz's zone. She follows the rooster with her gun **muzzle**. When the muzzle is just in front of the rooster, she pulls the trigger. The pheasant drops to the ground.

"I got it!" Liz yells. She picks up her empty shotgun shells so she doesn't litter. Ben lets Rex through the fence gate to **retrieve** the pheasant. Rex runs to the bird and picks it up in his mouth. Then he runs back to Liz, dropping the pheasant at her feet. Liz puts the bird into the large pocket on the back of her vest. Tonight, they'll have a tasty pheasant dinner.

Liz, Ben, and their dad are upland bird hunters. Upland game birds include pheasants, quail, and grouse. These birds live on dry upper land. Waterfowl game birds, such as ducks, live on lower ponds and rivers. The upland includes many bird habitats, from prairies to forests. For many years, people around the world have hunted upland birds for food and for fun.

To catch birds, hunters and their bird dogs must work together and be quick on their feet.

CHAPTER TWO

GETTING STARTED

To get started with upland bird hunting, hunters need to understand hunting rules and safety practices. Almost all US states require new hunters to take a hunter education class. These classes teach beginners how to identify different types of wildlife. They also teach people about hunting rules and safe gun handling. Learning these rules and skills helps people stay safe while hunting.

Hunters can find information about hunter education classes on state wildlife management websites. They can also find information about upland bird hunting mentorships. Mentorships pair students with experienced hunters who take them on their first hunt. Some state wildlife websites offer updated maps of public hunting areas, too. Hunters can use these maps to navigate land while hunting. If hunters want to hunt on private land, they must get permission from the landowners.

Beginners can practice handling guns at shooting ranges or hunter education classes. They learn how to aim accurately.

HUNTING ON CRP LAND

In 1985, the US Department of Agriculture started the Conservation Reserve Program (CRP). Farmers in this program receive government money to leave some of their farmland without crops for ten to 15 years. Instead, the farmers grow plants on the land that keep the soil healthy. This improves the environment by protecting water quality and wildlife habitats, including upland bird habitats. Many farmers make their CRP land available for upland bird hunting. CRP land is often a good place to hunt for upland birds such as pheasants, sharp-tailed grouse, and quail.

Hunters must also have the proper equipment. Upland bird hunters use shotguns, which shoot shotgun shells. These shells contain pellets that spread out as they leave the barrel of the gun. This makes it easier for hunters to hit fast-flying birds. Before shooting, hunters should quickly scan the area around them to make sure stray pellets will not harm other people or dogs.

Some bird hunters practice their aim by shooting clay discs. A device called a trap throws the discs into the air. Then hunters try to hit the discs with shot pellets before they reach the ground. To hit a moving target such as a bird, hunters learn to aim slightly in front of it. This is called wing shooting.

It's also important for hunters to wear the right clothing while hunting. Upland bird hunters often hike through prickly, wet, and rocky land to find upland birds. Wearing boots helps keep a hunter's feet dry and supported.

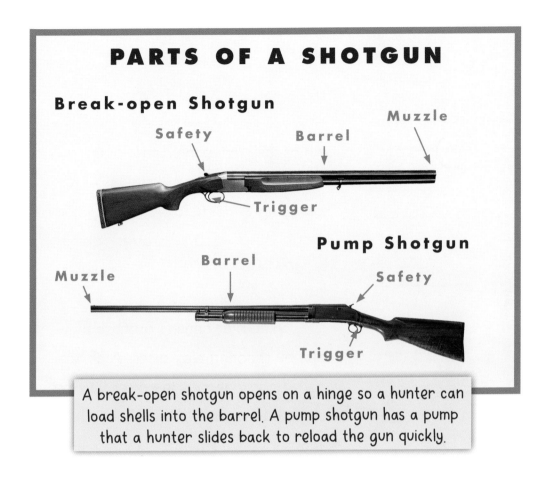

PARTS OF A SHOTGUN

Break-open Shotgun

Safety   Barrel   Muzzle

Trigger

Pump Shotgun

Muzzle   Barrel   Safety

Trigger

A break-open shotgun opens on a hinge so a hunter can load shells into the barrel. A pump shotgun has a pump that a hunter slides back to reload the gun quickly.

Brush pants, or coverings that go over pants, protect legs against thorny weeds and bushes. Dressing in layers helps hunters adapt to changing weather. Many hunters wear hunting vests with pockets that hold shotgun shells and birds. This way, a hunter can have both hands free to shoot. Wearing the right clothing can keep hunters safe, too. Safety glasses and earplugs protect a hunter's eyes and ears. Bright orange hats help hunters spot one another while out hunting. This helps prevent accidental shootings.

Some states require upland bird hunters to wear specific amounts of bright orange. This color is often called hunter orange or blaze orange.

Many upland bird hunters use bird dogs. These dogs use their excellent sense of smell to help hunters find game birds. Many bird dogs are also good at retrieving killed birds for a hunter. There are two main types of upland bird dogs. Flushing dogs help flush birds out of their hiding spots so hunters can shoot at them.

Pointing dogs hold still and point their noses toward birds. Then the hunter flushes the birds. For many hunters, watching their dogs find game birds is their favorite part of the hunt.

Flushing dogs work close within a hunter's range. They startle birds out of their hiding spots to make them fly into the air.

CHAPTER THREE

UPLAND BIRD CONSERVATION

Hunting for upland birds can be fun and exciting. But hunters also need to be responsible. Increasing **droughts**, modern farming methods, and growing cities are leaving upland birds with fewer places to live. Scientists, government organizations, and hunters work together to **conserve** upland birds and their habitats.

Scientists study game bird populations in different states. Many states have conservation organizations, such as a Department of Wildlife. These organizations use scientific information to make hunting rules. For instance, a state's wildlife management organization decides on the bag limit for each kind of upland bird in the state. The bag limit is the number of birds a hunter can shoot in a day without hurting that bird's population. Hunters can't shoot some female upland birds. In most states, only male pheasants can be hunted so females can lay more eggs.

Upland bird hunters must make sure they have permission to use land. If hunting on private land, hunters should check in with the landowner first. Following land regulations helps protect upland bird habitats.

USING DRONES TO STUDY NORTHERN BOBWHITE QUAIL

Scientists are researching new ways to help the northern bobwhite quail. This game bird's habitat and population are decreasing. Scientists use small drones to locate quail nests. They put temperature cameras on the drones. When the cameras sense a heat circle coming up from the ground, they are likely seeing a covey, or group of quail. Quail coveys sleep in a circle during winter to conserve heat and stay safe. Using drones to view nests helps scientists keep track of the quail population.

State wildlife management organizations also choose hunting seasons. Hunting season is the time of year when people are allowed to hunt a specific type of animal. To keep the bird population stable, birds must be able to peacefully nest and raise their young. Most birds do this in the spring. Because of this, the hunting season for most upland game birds is in the fall.

Hunters can support upland bird conservation by following the rules. Most states require hunters to buy hunting licenses. The money used to purchase licenses goes toward conservation projects. Hunters of all ages can help with these projects. For instance, hunters in the conservation group Pheasants Forever work with state wildlife organizations on habitat projects. They help landowners plant flowering plants. These plants attract insects that feed game bird chicks.

Some states require upland game bird hunters to report their kills. They must leave the bird's wing, leg, or head intact so it can be properly identified. This helps states keep track of bird populations.

Upland bird hunters can use the birds they hunt in many different ways. Many consider game birds a delicious meat source. There are many game bird recipes. Some hunters use game bird feathers to make fly fishing lures or art projects.

Some bullets used for hunting contain lead, which can be harmful to animals. Some states require all hunters to use nonlead shot when hunting upland game birds.

Experienced hunters can keep the tradition of upland game bird hunting alive by teaching beginners how to be responsible and respectful.

It takes time for beginners to gain the knowledge and skills needed for upland bird hunting. But with practice, upland bird hunting can be a safe and exciting way for hunters to enjoy the outdoors. By following hunting rules and respecting wildlife, hunters can help protect upland birds and their habitats for years to come.

FIND OUT MORE

IN THE LIBRARY

Kingston, Seth. *Hunting*. New York, NY: PowerKids Press, 2022.

Morey, Allan. *Hunting Dogs on the Job*.
Parker, CO: The Child's World, 2017.

Uhl, Xina M., and Jennifer Bringle. *Insider Tips for Wing Shooting*. New York, NY: Rosen Central, 2018.

ON THE WEB

Visit our website for links about upland bird hunting:
childsworld.com/links

Note to Parents, Caregivers, Teachers, and Librarians: We routinely verify our Web links to make sure they are safe and active sites. So encourage your readers to check them out!

INDEX